EAST RIDING
OF YORKSHIRE COUNCIL
Schools Library Service

PROJECT
April 2013

Materials

Rubber

Cassie Mayer

Heinemann LIBRARY

www.heinemann.co.uk/library
Visit our website to find out more information about Heinemann Library books.

To order:
 Phone 44 (0) 1865 888066
 Send a fax to 44 (0) 1865 314091
 Visit the Heinemann Bookshop at www.heinemann.co.uk/library to browse our
catalogue and order online.

First published in Great Britain by Heinemann Library,
Halley Court, Jordan Hill, Oxford OX2 8EJ, part of Pearson
Education. Heinemann is a registered trademark of Pearson
Education Ltd.

Editorial: Diyan Leake
Design: Joanna Hinton-Malivoire
Picture research: Tracy Cummins and Heather Mauldin
Production: Duncan Gilbert

Originated by Chroma Graphics (Overseas) Pte Ltd
Printed and bound in China by South China Printing Co. Ltd

ISBN 978 0 431 19261 1
12 11 10 09 08
10 9 8 7 6 5 4 3 2 1

British Library Cataloguing in Publication Dataassie.
Mayer, Cassie
 Rubber. - (Materials)
 1. Rubber - Juvenile literature
 I. Title
 620.1'94

Acknowledgments
The author and publisher are grateful to the following
for permission to reproduce copyright material: © Corbis
p. **15** (Remi Benali/Corbis); © Getty Images p. **7** (Richard
Drury); © Heinemann Raintree pp. **4**, **6**, **9**, **11**, **17**,
18, **19**, **20**, **21**, **22** (David Rigg); © Istockphoto p. **10**
(Justin Horrocks); © Peter Arnold p. **12** (Mark Edwards);
© Shutterstock pp. **5** (Geir Olav Lyngfjell), **8** (Perov
Stanislav), **13** (Cecilia Lim H M), **14** (Marco Rametta), **16**
(Feverpitched), **23** (Marco Rametta).

Cover image used with permission of © agefotostock
(Stephanie Adams). Back cover image used with
permission of © Heinemann Raintree (David Rigg).

Every effort has been made to contact copyright holders of
any material reproduced in this book. Any omissions will
be rectified in subsequent printings if notice is given to the
publisher.

Contents

What is rubber?

Rubber is a material.

People make rubber in factories.

People use rubber for lots of things.

Rubber can be thick.

Rubber can be thin.

Rubber can be hard.

Rubber can be soft.

Rubber can bounce.

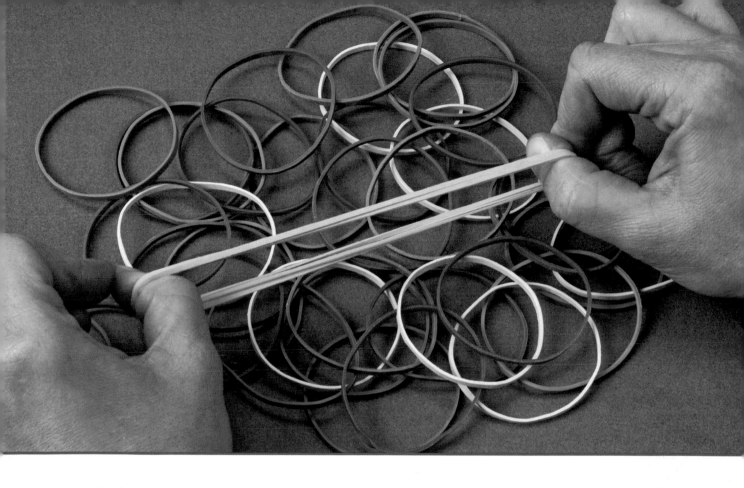

Rubber can stretch.

Making rubber

Some rubber is natural.

rubber tree

Natural rubber comes from
rubber trees.

The sap is taken from rubber trees.
It is made into rubber.

Some rubber is synthetic.

Synthetic rubber is made from oil.

How do people use rubber?

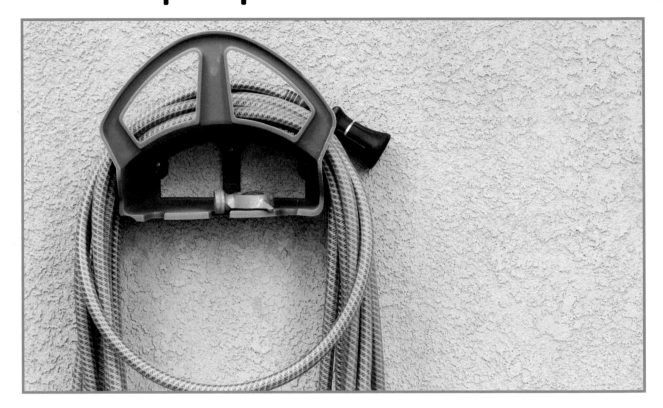

Rubber can be used to make hoses.

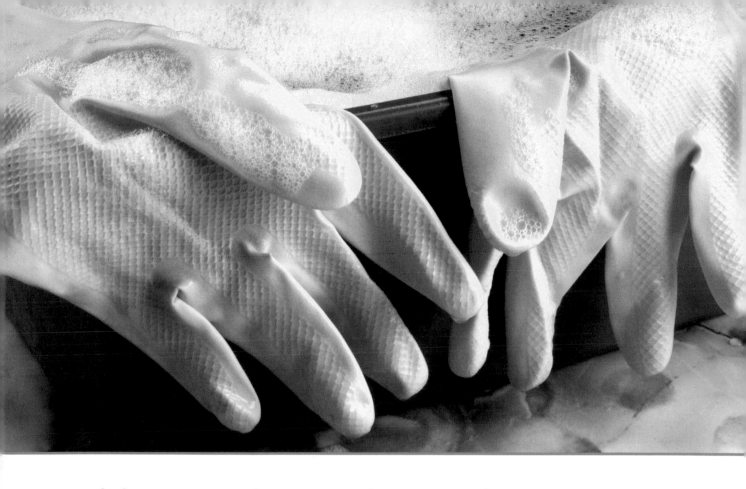

Rubber can be used to make gloves.

Rubber can be used to make tyres.

Rubber can be used to make toys.

Rubber can be used to make boots.

Rubber can be used to make lots
of things.

Things made of rubber

▲ tyres

▲ rubber erasers

▲ rubber toys

▲ rubber boots

Picture glossary

sap thick liquid that comes from trees

Content vocabulary for teachers

factory   building where goods are manufactured or assembled, mainly by machine

material   something that can be used to make things

natural   coming from plants, animals, or within the earth

synthetic   made to look as though it is a natural product

Index

Notes for parents and teachers

Before reading   Put items made of materials such as wood, plastic, metal, rock, and rubber in a closed bag. Challenge the children to feel in the bag and, without looking, identify the object made of rubber. What did it feel like? Was it cold to touch? Is it heavy? Was it squidgy? Talk about the properties of rubber.

After reading

• Show children some balloons. Encourage them to feel the balloons and talk about the texture. Pick up the balloons and drop them to the floor. What happens? Then inflate the balloons. What has happened to the size of the balloon? What happens now when they are dropped to the floor?

• In the hall or playground, show children a bouncy ball. See who can catch the ball after it has bounced. Contrast this with a cricket ball. Why does it not bounce?

• Help children to carefully stretch elastic bands over the base of an empty shoe box. Tell them to pluck the bands like strings of a guitar. What happens?